Searchlight BOOKS™

Space Mysteries

Mysteries of Deep Space

T0386561

Margaret J. Goldstein

Lerner Publications ◆ Minneapolis

Lerner Publications Company
An imprint of Lerner Publishing Group, Inc.
241 First Avenue North
Minneapolis, MN 55401 USA

For reading levels and more information, look up this title at www.lernerbooks.com.

Main body text set in Adrianna Regular 14/20.
Typeface provided by Chank.

Editor: Rebecca Higgins **Designer:** Mary Ross **Photo Editor:** Cynthia Zemlicka

Library of Congress Cataloging-in-Publication Data

Names: Goldstein, Margaret J., author.
Title: Mysteries of deep space / Margaret J. Goldstein.
Other titles: Searchlight books. Space mysteries.
Description: Minneapolis : Lerner Publications, [2021] | Series: Searchlight books — space mysteries | Includes bibliographical references and index. | Audience: Ages 8–11 | Audience: Grades 2–3 | Summary: "Could astronauts use wormholes to travel from galaxy to galaxy? Young readers can learn what scientists understand about the shape of space and other deep space mysteries"— Provided by publisher.
Identifiers: LCCN 2019055000 (print) | LCCN 2019055001 (ebook) | ISBN 9781541597419 (library binding) | ISBN 9781728413860 (paperback) | ISBN 9781728400877 (ebook)
Subjects: LCSH: Astronomy—Juvenile literature. | Cosmology—Juvenile literature.
Classification: LCC QB46 .G684 2021 (print) | LCC QB46 (ebook) | DDC 520—dc23

LC record available at https://lccn.loc.gov/2019055000
LC ebook record available at https://lccn.loc.gov/2019055001

Manufactured in the United States of America
1-47845-48285-3/13/2020

Contents

Chapter 1

MYSTERY PLANET

Billions of miles away from Earth, on the edges of our solar system, a mystery planet might be orbiting the sun. The planet might be as big as Neptune. It might take twenty thousand years to make just one trip around the sun.

If the planet is really out there, it's the ninth planet from the sun. So astronomers call it Planet Nine. But they don't know whether it exists or not.

This illustration shows Planet Nine orbiting far beyond all the other planets in our solar system.

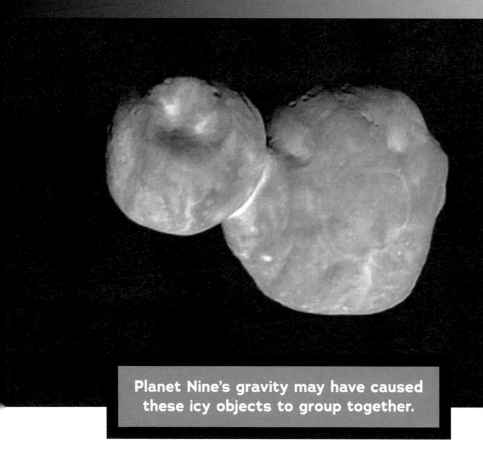

Planet Nine's gravity may have caused these icy objects to group together.

Astronomers at the California Institute of Technology first wrote about Planet Nine in 2015. They noticed that some rocky and icy objects in the Kuiper Belt, an area beyond Neptune, were grouped together. Astronomers thought that gravity from Planet Nine was pulling on the objects.

Since then, astronomers have been searching the edges of the solar system for Planet Nine. Unlike stars, planets don't give off light. So Planet Nine will be hard to find. But using powerful telescopes, astronomers might someday find the mystery planet.

The Great Unknown

Deep space is full of mysteries. How did the universe begin? Do aliens live on other planets? What happens when black holes collide? Using spacecraft and telescopes, scientists research answers to these questions and many more.

La Silla Observatory in Chile uses telescopes to explore the mysteries of deep space.

Chapter 2

OUTWARD BOUND

If you could travel to the end of the solar system, you would see Jupiter's red spot on your way. You would pass through the rings around Saturn. You'd fly through the icy Kuiper Belt. Then you'd reach the heliopause. This is like a boundary line around the solar system. Here is where the solar wind reaches its farthest limit. Once you passed this line, you'd be in interstellar space.

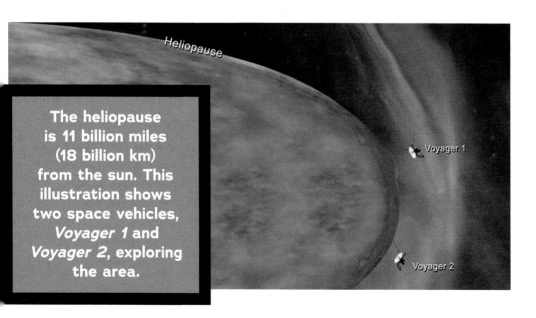

Heliopause

Voyager 1

Voyager 2

The heliopause is 11 billion miles (18 billion km) from the sun. This illustration shows two space vehicles, *Voyager 1* and *Voyager 2*, exploring the area.

Proxima Centauri is a red dwarf star, and its mass is an eighth of the sun's mass.

Room to Roam

Interstellar means "between stars." The space between stars is vast. For example, the nearest star to our sun, Proxima Centauri, is about 25 trillion miles (40 trillion km) away.

But interstellar space is not empty. It's filled with gas and dust. Sometimes the gas and dust swirl together into big clouds called nebulae. This is where new stars form.

Different kinds of energy, such as visible light waves, X-rays, gravitational waves, and radio waves, also travel through interstellar space. So do tiny, electrically charged particles called cosmic rays.

The star-forming region of this nebula is filled with hydrogen and other gases.

This illustration shows a collision between two rocky planets outside our solar system.

Sometimes meteors and comets zoom through interstellar space. Even some planets travel through interstellar space. They used to be in solar systems and orbited stars. But they left their orbits when violent events, such as collisions with other planets, flung them into interstellar space.

STEM Spotlight

Scientists have sent many spacecraft to explore our solar system. The two *Voyager* spacecraft, launched in 1977, studied Jupiter, Saturn, Uranus, and Neptune. Then they continued to the outer reaches of the solar system. *Voyager 1* left the solar system in 2012. *Voyager 2* left in 2018. The spacecraft are still measuring and monitoring energy and particles in interstellar space. They still send radio signals back to astronomers on Earth. In case alien beings ever find one of the *Voyagers*, both spacecraft carry visual and sound messages about Earth and its living things.

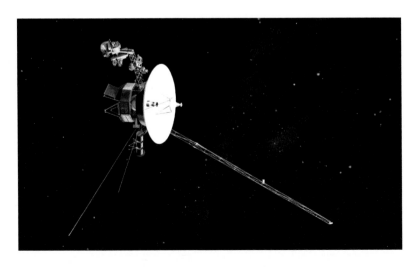

Chapter 3

WORLDS BEYOND

Imagine a planet with rocky ground, deep oceans full of water, and sunny skies. The planet is not too hot or too cold for living things. The air contains life-giving gases. Millions of plants and animals live there.

Scientists are looking for another planet with water and breathable air.

MARS HAS DRIED-UP RIVERS. THESE RIVERS MAY HAVE SUPPORTED LIFE.

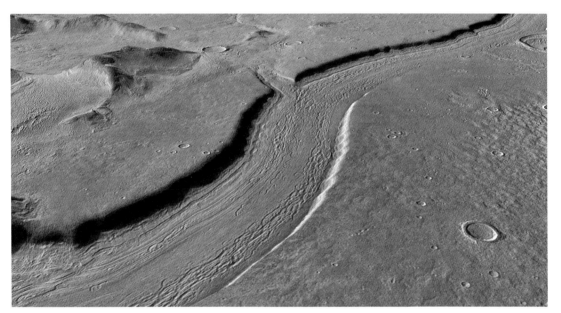

That sounds like Earth. But there might be another planet, somewhere in the universe, similar to Earth. Maybe the planet has some of the ingredients that support life on Earth, such as water.

The universe has trillions of solar systems like ours. It has trillions of planets. Some of them might have life too. Astronomers want to find these planets.

Astronomers have found thousands of exoplanets and are looking for more. The James Webb Space Telescope will scan the universe for exoplanets. It will launch in 2021.

But exoplanets are hard to find because planets don't give off light. So astronomers look for clues that a planet is orbiting a star. For example, a little wobble in a star's orbit could mean that a planet's gravity is pulling at the star. If a star grows dim for a time, a planet might be crossing in front of it, blocking some of the star's light.

The James Webb Space Telescope will look for signs of water on exoplanets.

Even though astronomers know how to find exoplanets, finding life on exoplanets will be much harder. Exoplanets are too far away to visit with spacecraft. Even the best telescopes can't see them clearly. They are too small, too dark, and too far away.

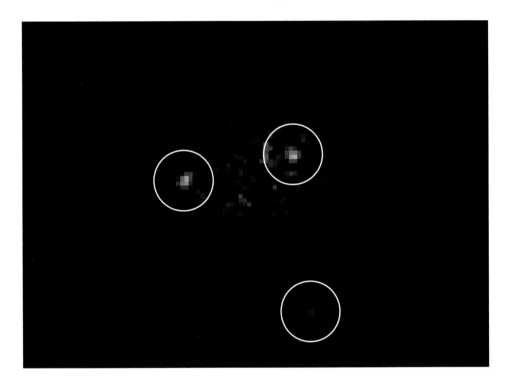

IT'S DIFFICULT TO GET PICTURES OF EXOPLANETS, BUT ASTRONOMERS USED THIS IMAGE TO DISCOVER THREE EXOPLANETS.

A supermassive black hole has more mass than a million suns.

Galaxies Galore

A galaxy is a giant system with billions of stars and other space objects. Each galaxy has a supermassive black hole at its center. This is an area where gravity is so great that nothing can escape, not even light.

The universe has billions of galaxies. Our galaxy is called the Milky Way. If you could see the Milky Way from above, it would look like a pinwheel. You would see a big bulge of stars in the middle and long curving arms made of stars around the outside. Astronomers call it a spiral galaxy.

Spiral galaxies are the most common type of galaxy in the universe.

Outside and Between

Intergalactic space is the region between galaxies. This space contains gases, light, and other kinds of energy. It also holds stars that have left their galaxies. They were probably knocked into intergalactic space when two galaxies collided. Some scientists think that half the stars in the universe are intergalactic stars.

THIS BLUE STAR WAS KNOCKED
INTO INTERGALATIC SPACE AFTER COMING
CLOSE TO A BLACK HOLE.

Even without a telescope, you can see other galaxies—including Andromeda—on clear nights.

How big is intergalactic space? The distances are hard to imagine. Even if you could travel at the speed of light, it would still take 2.54 million years to get from the Milky Way to the nearest spiral galaxy, Andromeda.

STEM Spotlight

Sometimes two or more galaxies collide and merge. During the collision, the supermassive black holes at the galaxies' centers swirl together. The event sends powerful gravitational waves rippling through the universe. The merger can take millions of years to complete. When it's done, the merged galaxy might have a new shape, with an even larger supermassive black hole at the center.

Chapter 4

COSMIC FORCES

Astronomers think the universe began about 13.8 billion years ago. At that time, all matter, space, and energy were packed into a single tiny point. In an event called the big bang, that point suddenly expanded. Right after the big bang, the universe contained only tiny particles. Over time, these particles combined to form gases, dust, stars, planets, and galaxies.

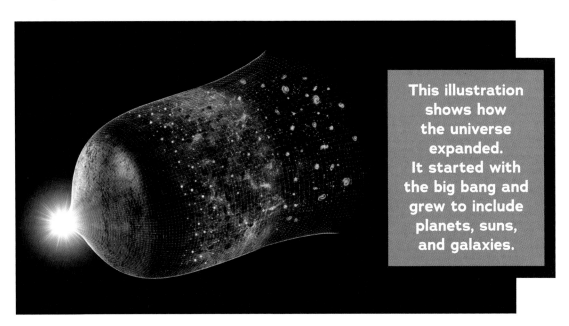

This illustration shows how the universe expanded. It started with the big bang and grew to include planets, suns, and galaxies.

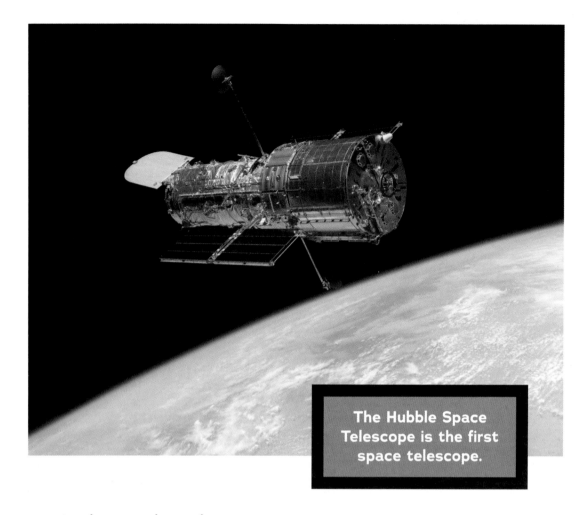

The Hubble Space Telescope is the first space telescope.

Looking Backward

The Hubble Space Telescope has seen back in time. For example, in 2016 the Hubble spied a galaxy called GN-z11. This galaxy is about 13.3 billion light-years away from us. That means that light from GN-z11 traveled for about 13.3 billion years to reach Earth. So Hubble saw the galaxy as it looked more than 13 billion years ago, not as it looks now.

GN-z11 is one of the oldest galaxies ever discovered. It was around when the universe was very young. By studying GN-z11 and other old galaxies, astronomers can better understand the creation of the universe. New telescopes might let us see an even younger universe. Someday, we might even see all the way back to the big bang.

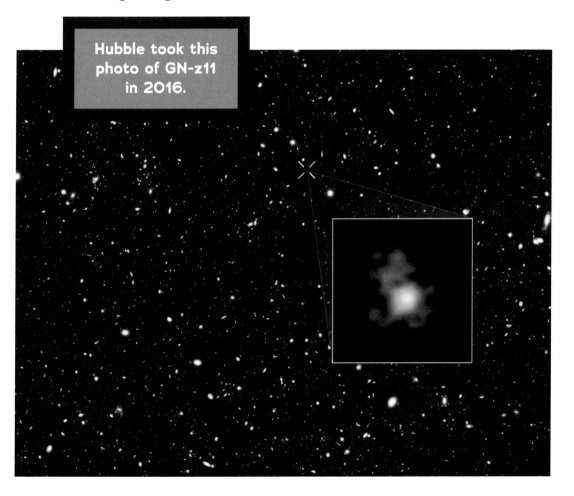

Hubble took this photo of GN-z11 in 2016.

Space Fact or Fiction?

We can use wormholes to speed up space travel.

This is fiction. Wormhole travel is based on the theory that the universe is curved into a U shape. If this theory were true, perhaps a spacecraft could travel through a wormhole, or tunnel, between the straight parts of the U. In this way the craft could get through space much more quickly than if it had to travel along the curve of the U. The idea that the universe is curved is just a theory, however. Scientists have found no evidence that wormholes really exist.

The Andromeda galaxy has about one trillion stars.

The Dark Side

All galaxies spin. In the 1970s, astronomers at the Carnegie Institution in Washington, DC, were studying the Andromeda galaxy. They saw that the stars in the outer arms of the spiral moved through space just as fast as stars at the center. According to the laws of gravity, the outer stars should have been moving

ASTRONOMER VERA RUBIN DISCOVERED DARK MATTER.

Astronomers thought the gravity of something unknown was pulling on the edges of galaxies. This unknown material didn't give off any light, so it was invisible. Astronomers called the substance dark matter.

Many scientists think that dark matter is made mostly of tiny particles. The particles are called weakly interacting massive particles, or WIMPs. Scientists think dark matter makes up more than 80 percent of the matter in the universe.

The Dark Side, Part 2

Ever since the big bang, the universe has been expanding. Galaxies are moving farther away from one another. Twentieth-century astronomers thought that gravity would slow the expansion of the universe. But pictures from the Hubble Space Telescope show that the expansion is speeding up, not slowing down. Astronomers think a mysterious force is working against gravity and speeding up the expansion of the universe. They call this force dark energy.

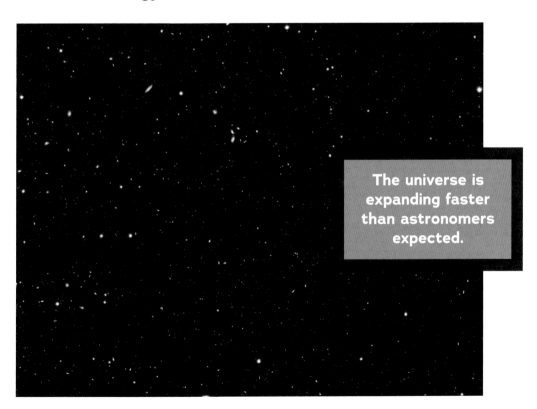

The universe is expanding faster than astronomers expected.

Astronomers are still studying
dark energy and dark matter.

Scientists think that dark energy makes up about
68 percent of the universe. What exactly is dark energy?
Scientists don't know. This is one of the many mysteries
of deep space that remains to be solved.

3D Printer Activity

With the Hubble Space Telescope, astronomers have been able to see distant stars and galaxies. The Hubble has looked back into the early universe and also helped scientists learn about dark energy. You can make a 3D-printed model of the Hubble by visiting the link below.

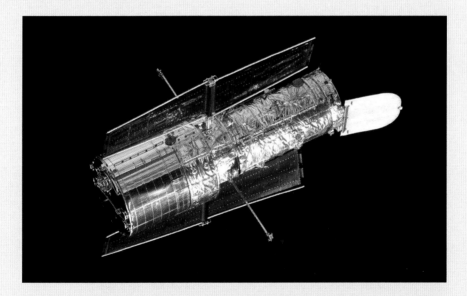

PAGE
PLUS

https://qrs.lernerbooks.com/Hubble-25

Glossary

astronomer: a scientist who studies the universe and the objects in it

black hole: an area of space with so much gravity that nothing can escape from it

exoplanet: a planet outside our solar system

gravitational wave: a type of energy created by violent events, such as the collision of two black holes

gravity: an invisible force that attracts stars, planets, and other space objects to one another

matter: the material an object is made of

orbit: to travel around something. The path one object takes around another is also called its orbit

solar system: a star and the planets and other objects orbiting around it

solar wind: particles that flow from the sun to the very edges of the solar system

speed of light: the speed at which light travels, which is 186,282 miles (299,792 km) per second

supermassive black hole: a black hole with more mass, or matter, than a million suns

Learn More about the Mysteries of Deep Space

Books

Peterson, Christy. *Cutting-Edge Hubble Telescope Data.* Minneapolis: Lerner Publications, 2020.

> The Hubble Space Telescope lets astronomers peer back billions of years. Find out more about this groundbreaking telescope.

Rathburn, Betsy. *Galaxies.* Minneapolis: Bellwether Meda, 2019

> Learn about galaxy shapes, galaxy mergers, and more.

Simon, Seymour. *Exoplanets.* New York: Harper, 2018.

> Simon explores the mysteries of exoplanets.

Websites

The Big Bang

> https://www.esa.int/kids/en/learn/Our_Universe/Story_of_the_Universe/The_Big_Bang
>
> Dive deep into the big bang theory—the idea that the universe began with the expansion of a single tiny point.

Dark Matter

> https://spaceplace.nasa.gov/dark-matter/en/
>
> NASA introduces dark matter, a mysterious substance that pulls on galaxies.

Wormholes

> https://www.ouruniverseforkids.com/worm-holes/
>
> What if space were curved and you could take a tunnel from one side of the curve to the other? Explore the idea of wormholes.

Index

Photo Acknowledgments

Wikimedia Commons/Nagualdesign/Tom Ruen/background from ESO (CC BY-SA 4.0), p. 4; NASA/ Johns Hopkins University Applied Physics Laboratory/Southwest Research Institute, p. 5; ESO/B. Tafreshi (twanight.org), p. 6; NASA/JPL/Caltech, p. 7; NASA/ESA/Hubble, p. 8; Nathan Smith, University of Minnesota/NOAO/AURA/NSF, p. 9; NASA/SOFIA/Lynette Cook, p. 10; NASA/JPL, p. 11; Anton Petrus/Getty Images, p. 12; ESA/DLR/FU Berlin/G. Neukum (CC BY-SA 3.0 IGO), p. 13; Northrup Grumman, p. 14; NASA, ESA, and R. Soummer (STScI), p. 15; ESO/M. Kornmesser, p. 16; NASA/ESA/Judy Schmidt, p. 17; NASA/ESA/G. Bacon (STScI), p. 18; idizimage/Getty Images, p. 19; ALMA (ESO/NAOJ/NRAO). Visible light image: the NASA/ESA Hubble, p. 20; Nicolle R. Fuller/NSF, p. 21; NASA, p. 22; NASA, ESA, P. Oesch (Yale University), G. Brammer (STScI), P. van Dokkum (Yale University), and G. Illingworth (University of California, Santa Cruz), p. 23; Mark Garlick/Science Photo Library/Getty Images, p. 24; X-ray: NASA/CXC/ITA/INAF/J.Merten et al, Lensing: NASA/ STScI; NAOJ/Subaru; ESO/VLT, Optical: NASA/STScI/R.Dupke, p. 25; NSF's National Optical-Infrared Astronomy Research Laboratory/KPNO/AURA, p. 26; NASA, ESA, G. Illingworth and D. Magee (University of California, Santa Cruz), K. Whitaker (University of Connecticut), R. Bouwens (Leiden University), P. Oesch (University of Geneva), and the Hubble Legacy Field team, p. 27; NASA, ESA, E. Jullo (JPL/LAM), P. Natarajan (Yale) and J-P. Kneib (LAM), p. 28; NASA, ESA, G. Illingworth and D. Magee (University of California, Santa Cruz), K. Whitaker (University of Connecticut), R. Bouwens (Leiden University), P. Oesch (University of Geneva), and the Hubble Legacy Field team, p. 29.

Cover: Mark Garlick/Science Photo Library/Getty Images.